PIANO
Adventures®

Arranged by Nancy and Randall Faber

THE BASIC PIANO METHOD

Production Coordinator: Jon Ophoff
Cover and Illustrations: Terpstra Design, San Francisco
Engraving: Dovetree Productions, Inc.
Editors: Edwin McLean and Joanne Smith

FABER
PIANO ADVENTURES®
3042 Creek Drive
Ann Arbor, Michigan 48108

ISBN 978-1-61677-290-1

A Note to Teacher and Parents

For decades, popular repertoire has captured the hearts of people worldwide. Perhaps it is the memorable melodies, engaging lyrics, and catchy rhythms that create its magic and universal appeal. Some of America's finest music makers have left us a legacy that will be treasured for all time—Jerry Bock's *Sunrise, Sunset* from *Fiddler on the Roof*; George Gershwin's *I Got Rhythm*; and Elton John's *Honky Cat*.

Piano Adventures® Popular Repertoire (Level 3B) offers a unique teaching experience for teacher and student alike. Outstanding popular repertoire has been skillfully arranged and correlated with the concepts in the Piano Adventures® Lesson Book (Level 3B). A notable feature of *Piano Adventures® Popular Repertoire* is the fun-filled activity page that follows each popular selection. At Level 3B, these pages imaginatively engage the student in harmony, ear training, rhythmic study, sightreading, and the understanding of musical terms. A music dictionary at the end of the book provides a quick and easy reference for basic musical terms.

So have fun! America's finest popular repertoire has now been pedagogically presented with what many are calling the finest method ever—*Piano Adventures®*!

CONTENTS

The Rose

Words and Music by
Amanda McBroom

FF129

DISCOVERY Where is the melody played by the *R.H.*? Where does it return to the *L.H.*?

Which do you hear?

- Your teacher will play **example a** or **b**.
- Listen carefully and circle the example you hear.

The Rose

Words and Music by
Amanda McBroom

Extra Credit: Play each example above.

I'll Be There for You

Words by
David Crane, Marta Kauffman,
Allee Willis, Phil Solem, and Danny Wilde

Key of _____ Major

Music by
Michael Skloff

Brightly

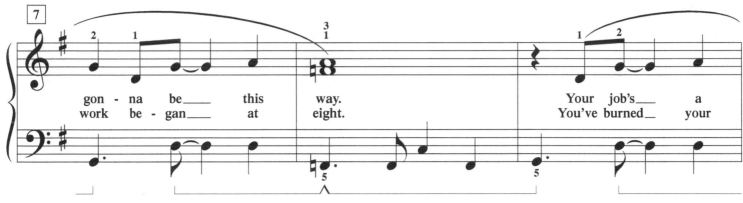

So no___ one told you life___ was
You're still___ in bed at ten___ and

gon - na be___ this way.
work be - gan___ at eight.

Your job's___ a
You've burned___ your

joke, you're broke;___ your love life's D. O. A.
break - fast; so___ far ev - 'ry - thing is great.

FF129

It's like____ you're al - ways stuck in sec - ond gear,____
Your moth - er warned you there'd be days like these,____

and it has - n't been____ your day, your week,____ your
but she did - n't tell____ you when the world____ has

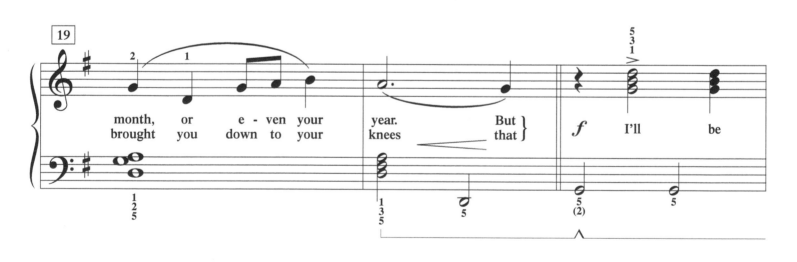

month, or e - ven your year. But that
brought you down to your knees

f I'll be

there for____ you____ when the rain starts____ to

25

fall. I'll be there for____ you,____ like I've

28

been there____ be - fore. I'll be there for____ you,____

31

1.

'cause you're there for____ me, too.____

35

2.

too.

rit.

DISCOVERY

Name the two **major chord harmonies** used from *measures 1–11*.

____ Major and ____ Major

Name the **minor chord harmony** at *measure 12*. ____ minor

An Offbeat Occurrence

Syncopation—change from the normal pattern of accent. Instead of accenting the strong beats of the measure, the accent occurs *between* the beats—on the *offbeats*.

- Play these examples, counting aloud.

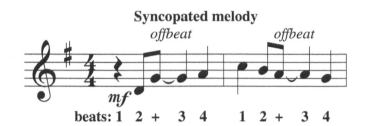

The examples below use **syncopation**.

- Write the counts **1 2 3 4** under the main beats. For notes between the beats, write **+** (for "and").

- Circle the *offbeat* where the syncopation occurs.

- Tap (or clap) each measure, counting aloud.

- Then play, counting aloud.

I'll Be There for You

Music by
Michael Skloff

1.

2.

3.

4.

5.

6.

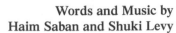

Inspector Gadget
(Main Theme)

Words and Music by
Haim Saban and Shuki Levy

Lively, with swing (♫ = ♩ ♪)

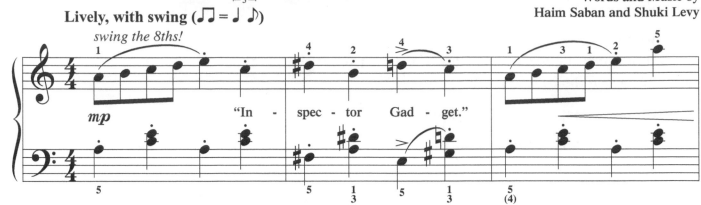

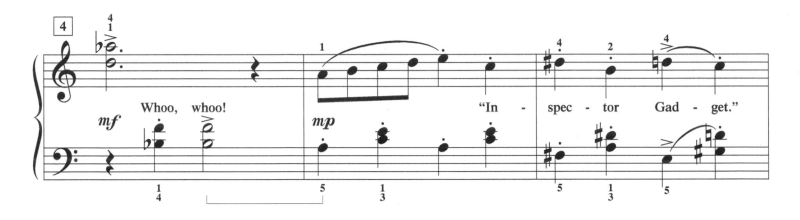

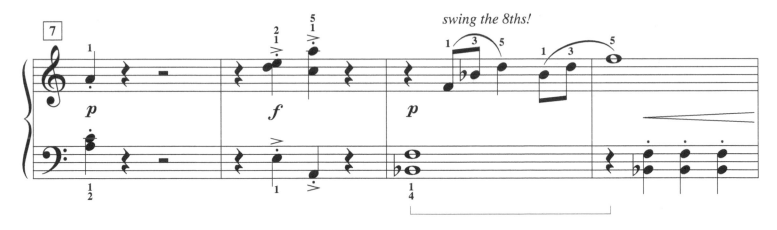

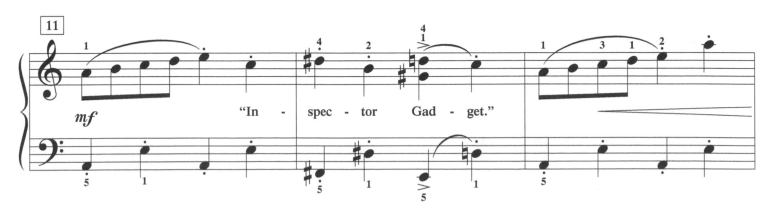

FF1290

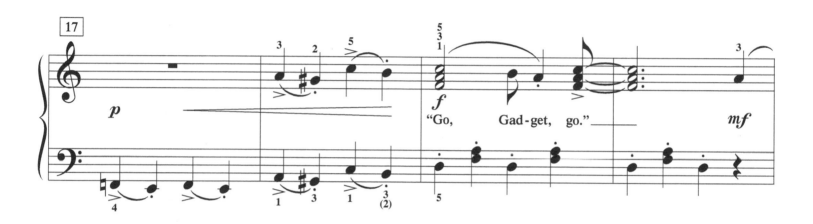

D I S C O V E R Y

Name the scale used from *measures 39–41*.

Inspector Swing

Swing Review:
If the *tempo mark* includes the word "swing,"
play the 8th notes with a *long-short* swing rhythm.

Swing Study

Extra Credit: Play *Swing Study* at these tempos:

    Slow ♩ = 100   **Moderate** ♩ = 120   **Fast** ♩ = 160

The Imperial March
(Darth Vader's Theme)

from *Star Wars: The Empire Strikes Back*

Music by John Williams

Heavy march, in two (♩ = 92)

FF129

DISCOVERY In *measures 25-29,* is the L.H. playing the **tonic** or **dominant** note?

Transposition Star

- Name the key for each example.
- Then sightread the phrases below.

The Imperial March

Music by John Williams

Heavy march, in two   Key of ____ Minor

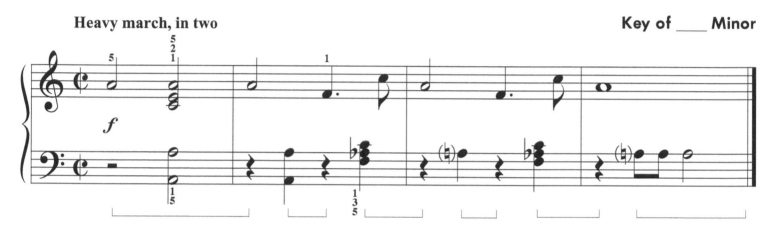

Heavy march, in two   Key of ____ Minor

Heavy march, in two   Key of ____ Minor

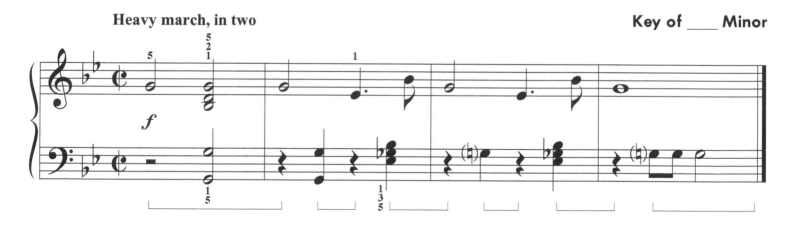

Jeopardy Theme

Key of _____ Major

Music by
Merv Griffin

Cheerfully

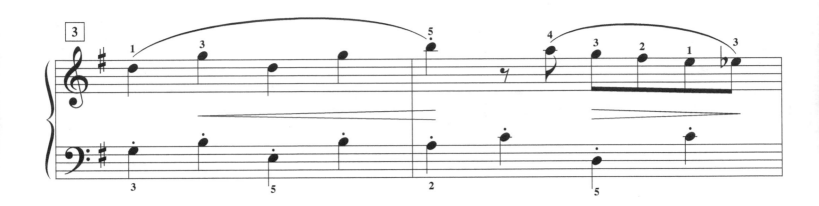

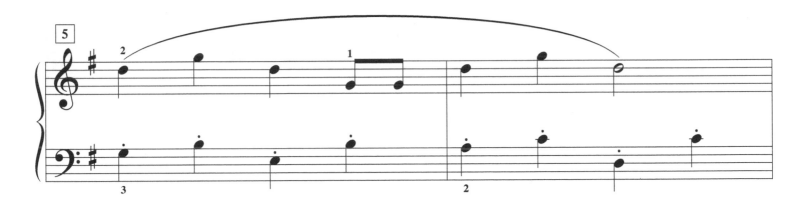

Key change to D major

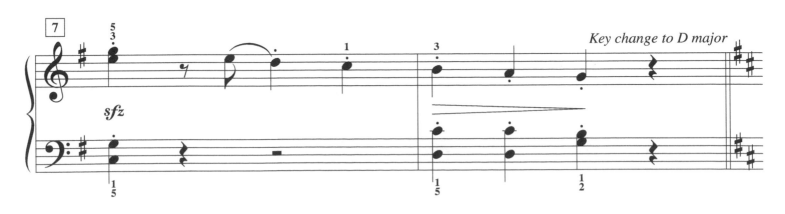

FF1290

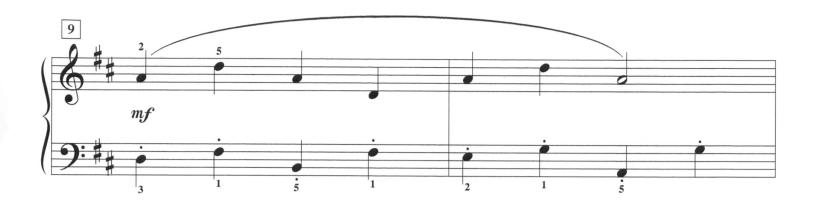

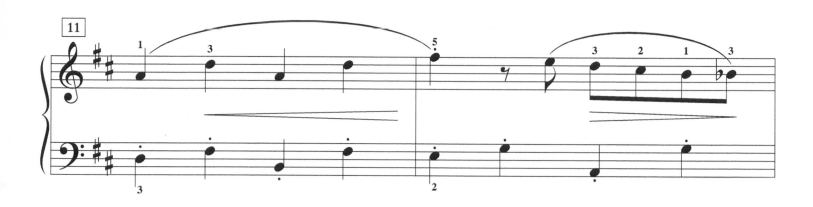

DISCOVERY In the opening three measures, the R.H. uses only: *(circle one)*

dominant and **leading tone** notes   **dominant** and **tonic** notes

Triads in Jeopardy

- Name the R.H. intervals in the boxes for the first example. (**2nd**, **3rd**, **4th**, **5th**, etc.)
- Then play the opening measures of *Jeopardy* in all 12 keys!

Jeopardy Theme

Music by
Merv Griffin

FF1290

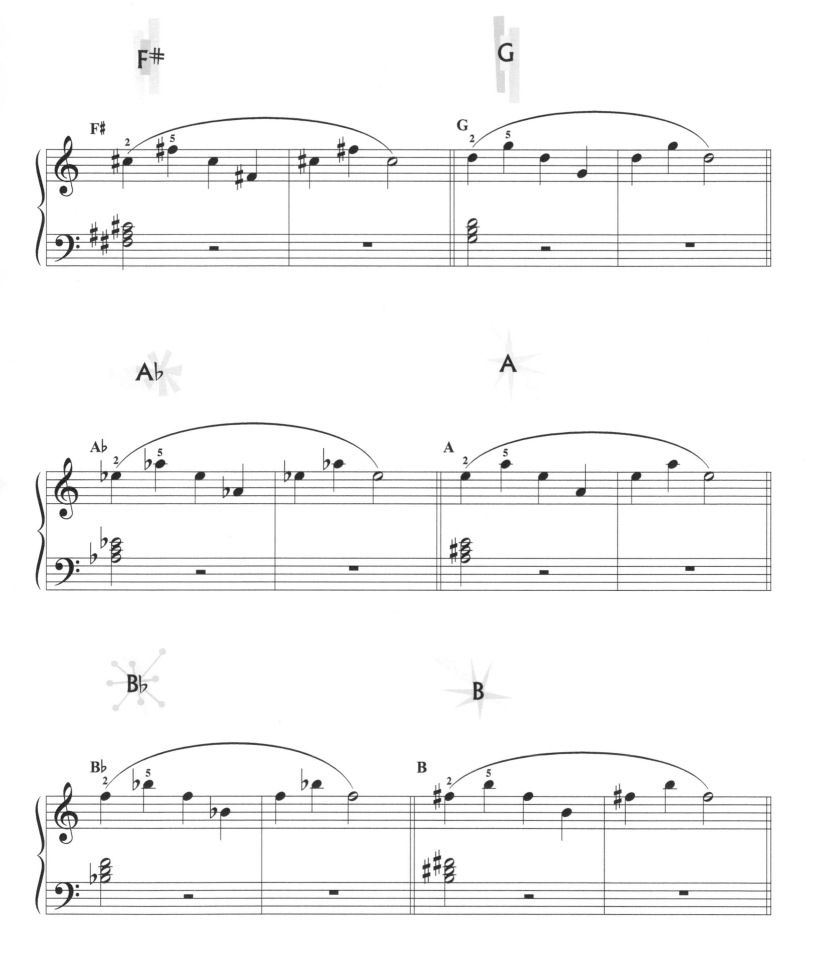

Extra Credit: Repeat this exercise with the R.H. playing each quarter note *staccato*.

Angel Eyes

Composed by
Jim Brickman

Flowing gently

FF1290

Point out two **sevenths** for the R.H.

FF1290

LEAD SHEET

Triad Accompaniment

Review: A **lead sheet** is the melody only, with chord symbols written above to show the harmony.

• First play the melody alone with your R.H.

• Then add L.H. *blocked chords* as indicated by the chord symbols.

sightreading

Angel Eyes

Composed by
Jim Brickman

Extra Credit: Your teacher may coach you to play some of the chords in **1st** or **2nd inversion**.
(This will keep your L.H. from making leaps between **root position** triads.)

Sunrise, Sunset
from *FIDDLER ON THE ROOF*

Lyrics by Sheldon Harnick

Music by Jerry Bock

Moderately slow waltz

mp

Is this the lit - tle girl I car -
When did she grow to be a beau -

ried?
ty?

Is this the lit - tle boy at play?
When did he grow to be so tall?

I don't re - mem - ber grow - ing old -
Was - n't it yes - ter - day when old they

er.
When did they?

mf

rit.

FF1290

were small? Sun - rise, sun - set. Sun - rise, sun - set,

Swift - ly flow the days.

Seed - lings turn o - ver - night to sun - flowers,

blos - som - ing e - ven as we gaze.

rit.

a tempo

DISCOVERY

Point out a *grace note*. How is it played?

One chord following another . . .

- Write the chord symbol for each measure in the box given.
  major chord—capital letter (Ex. **C**)
  minor chord—capital letter plus lower-case "m" (Ex. **Em**)

- Then play, saying the chord names aloud.

Sunset Etude

based on music by Jerry Bock

Moderately slow

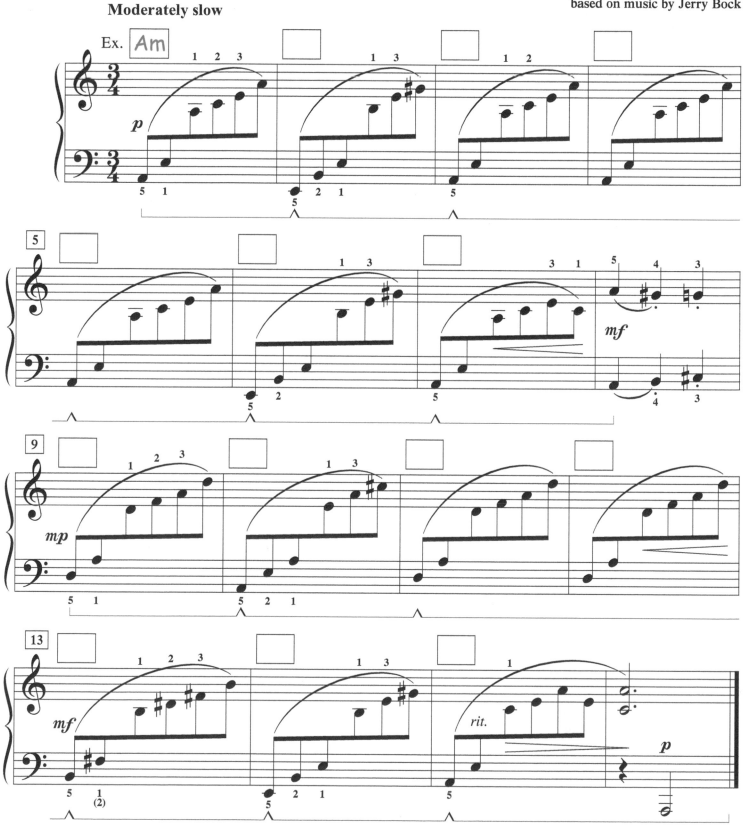

Honky Cat

Words and Music by
Elton John and Bernie Taupin

FF1290

bop-pin' in the coun - try, fish - in' in a stream,

look - in' for an an - swer,

tryin' to find___ a sign.___ Un - til I saw your

cit - y lights,___ hon - ey, I___ was blind. They said,

Lyrics under the staff:

f "Get back, hon - ky cat, better get back to the

woods." Well, I quit those days and___ my red - neck

ways and___ a, oo, oo, oo, oo,___ *ff* oh, the change___
cresc.

___ is gon - na do me good.

1. **2.**
f *f* *rit.*

8va⎤

Point out at least five examples of *syncopation*.

"... lookin' for an answer"

Honky Cat

Words and Music by
Elton John and Bernie Taupin

Complete the information for each example from *Honky Cat*.

1. Does the L.H. begin on the **tonic** or **dominant** note? *(circle one)*

2. What is the position of these R.H. chords?

root position   **1st inversion**   **2nd inversion**

(circle one)

3. This *offbeat* rhythm in the R.H. is called _____.

4. Circle the *offbeat* where the syncopation occurs.

5. Name the three accidentals.

____, ____, and ____

6. Name the L.H. interval.

I Got Rhythm

Music and Lyrics by
George and Ira Gershwin

FF1290

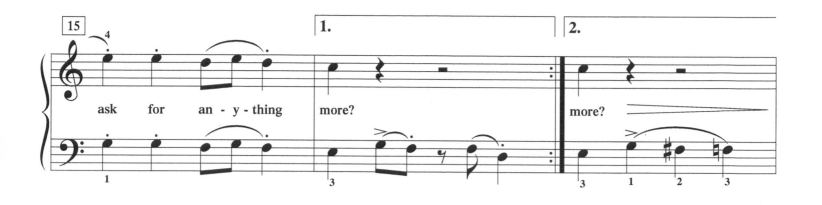

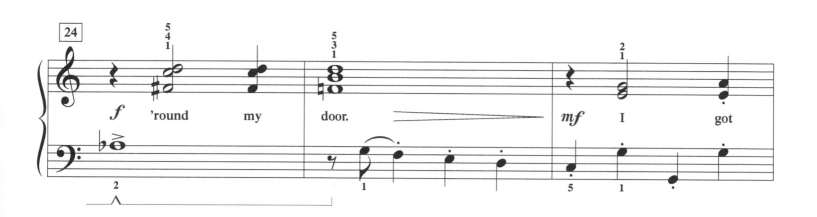

star - light.____ I got sweet dreams.____

I got my man.____ Who could ask for an - y - thing

more? Who could ask for an - y - thing more?

DISCOVERY *I Got Rhythm* uses this two-measure rhythm pattern: $\frac{4}{4}$ ♩ ♩ ♩ ♩ ♩. ♩ ♩
Point out at least eight examples of this rhythm for the R.H.

  FF1290

I Got Endings

- Play each "new" ending for *I Got Rhythm*. You may enjoy substituting one of these endings at *measure 35*.

- Can you make up your own ending?

I Got Rhythm

Music and Lyrics by
George and Ira Gershwin

Alternate Ending 1

Alternate Ending 2

Alternate Ending 3

(you write)

MUSIC DICTIONARY

pp	*p*	*mp*	*mf*	*f*	*ff*
pianissimo	**piano**	**mezzo piano**	**mezzo forte**	**forte**	**fortissimo**
very soft	soft	medium soft	medium loud	loud	very loud

crescendo (cresc.)
Play gradually louder.

diminuendo (dim.) or decrescendo (decresc.)
Play gradually softer.

SIGN	TERM	DEFINITION
	accent mark	Play this note louder.
	accidental	A sharp or flat that is not in the key signature. A natural is also an accidental.
	accompaniment	The harmony and rhythm that accompany the melody.
	arpeggio	The notes of a chord played up or down the keyboard.
	a tempo	Return to the beginning tempo (speed).
	blocked chord	The notes of a chord played together.
	broken chord	The notes of a chord played separately.
	chord	Three or more notes sounding together.
	chord analysis	Naming the chord letter names (Ex. Dm) or the Roman numerals (Ex. I, IV, V7, etc.) of a piece.
	chord symbol	The letter name of the chord indicated above the music. A lowercase "m" is used to show minor.
	chord tone	One of the notes of a chord.
	chorus	A repeated section (music and lyrics) of a song that often features the words of the title.
	chromatic scale	A 12-note scale composed only of half steps.
	dominant	Step 5 of the scale.
	dynamics	The "louds and softs" of music. See dynamic marks above.
	fermata	Hold this note longer than its usual value.
	half step	The distance from one key to the very closest key on the keyboard. (Ex. C-C♯ or E-F)
	interval	The distance between two musical tones or keys on the keyboard. For example, 2nd, 3rd, 4th, 5th, octave.
	inversion	A rearrangement of the tones of a chord. The 3rd is in the bass for 1st inversion; the 5th is in the bass for 2nd inversion. (See root position.)
	key signature	Sharps or flats of the key. The key signature appears at the beginning of each line of music.

FF1290